LADY COTTINGTON'S PRESSED FAIRY BOOK

Turner Publishing, Inc.

ATLANTA

Published by Turner Publishing, Inc.
A Subsidiary of Turner Broadcasting System, Inc.
1050 Techwood Drive, N.W.
Atlanta, Georgia 30318

Distributed by Andrews and McMeel
A Universal Press Syndicate Company
4900 Main Street
Kansas City, Missouri 64112

ISBN 1-57036-062-6

10 9 8 7 6 5 4 3

First published in Great Britain in 1994 by
Pavilion Books Limited

Designed by Wherefore Art?
Calligraphy by Ruth Rowland

Printed and bound in Italy by Graphicom

Turner Publishing, Inc.

PUBLISHER'S NOTE

The RSPCF (The Royal Society for the Prevention of Cruelty to Fairies) has asked the publisher to make it clear that no fairies were injured or killed during the manufacturing of this book. The pictures in this book are *psychic impressions* of fairies. The RSPCF would also like to point out that, after one or two unfortunate casualties in the early stages, all the fairies presented in these pages had discovered a way of leaving their psychic imprint without suffering any physical harm themselves. In fact, the whole process became recognized as a *Fairy Sporting Activity* and qualified for a Gooseberry Medal at the Millennial Fairy Olympics in 1921.

Of course everyone is familiar with the famous photograph of the small girl surrounded by fairies, which caused such a sensation when it was first published in *The Regular* magazine in 1907. It inspired many imitations and was circulated around the world. While some sceptics dismissed it as a hoax, it was hailed in many quarters as the final, irrefutable proof of the existence of fairies. No less an authority on the subject than Sir Arthur Conan Doyle was fully persuaded of its authenticity, and spoke to packed audiences about its significance, particularly in the Manchester area. J. M. Barrie himself was convinced that he recognized at least one of the fairies in the photograph, and the Rev. Charles Dodgson (better known as Lewis Carroll) appeared from beyond the grave to clairvoyants up and down the country to vouch for the veracity of the photograph.

But, until recently, surprisingly little was known about the young girl in the photograph. It was known that her name was Angelica Cottington, and that she was the only daughter of Lord Cottington of Bovey, but otherwise the page of history upon which her name appears was blank. On the death of her father, Angelica became Lady Cottington, and lived as a recluse on the family estate until she died in 1991. She never married and had no friends or even acquaintances other than her housekeeper, Ethel, and she did not even know her very well.

It was thought that perhaps it was the ridicule heaped upon the photos by the popular press that drove Angelica Cottington into her life of seclusion. But nobody really knew the full story, until last year, when the Cottington estate was bought by Potterton Properties plc, and the old house was finally demolished to make way for a Prestige Office Block in an unspoilt country setting, which so many firms have already chosen as their preferred lifestyle.

Before the bulldozers moved in, a group of local trouble-makers, led by the vicar, the Rev. Charles Dodgson (no relation), Dr Broadbent (Bovey's last GP working within the now outmoded NHS system) and the entire population of the village of Bovey itself, established a squat in the building with the intention of preventing Potterton Properties plc from going about their lawful business of obliterating the Elizabethan manor house and medieval outbuildings. During the course of this occupation (which was eventually brought to a conclusion by the police and the armed forces, with surprisingly little loss of life) one of the squatters, the Right Hon. Phillip Menzies, MP, QC, OBE, discovered a small volume stuck behind a trunk in the attic.

As he was about to tear out the pages in order to light a fire, he became aware that he might be holding in his hands something rather special. When he put his glasses on, he immediately recognized the importance of his find. He abandoned the squat in order to obtain the services of a first-class London lawyer, who specialized in *Copyright, Treasure Trove* and *Making Money out of Other People's Property* (a little-known by-water of English law, which has proved surprisingly fruitful for those who have taken the trouble to avail themselves of it).

Thanks to this chance discovery, and the untiring efforts of the publicity department of the publisher, you are now holding in your hands a faithful reproduction of one of the most intriguing, sensational and epoch-making books of all times – *Lady Cottington's Pressed Fairy Book.*

Here at last is explained – in all its graphic detail – the way in which that first photograph came to be taken. What is more, here is a faithful record of many, many more fairies who appeared to Angelica Cottington throughout her earliest years. And not only written accounts – for this book is nothing less than a physical record of actual living fairies.

The way in which all of these remarkable impressions came to be left upon these pages is explained within the book itself, and in a further batch of photographs which was later found under her bed. Suffice it to say that Angelica Cottington discovered that if she sat still with the book upon her lap, fairies (being inquisitive creatures) would come fluttering around her, and with a sure eye, a quick lunge

and a firm snapping together of the book she could catch the fairies between her pages and thus preserve their appearance for posterity.

At the same time, Lady Cottington kept a detailed diary of her fairy sightings and this is faithfully reproduced here in its original position, alongside the pressings of the fairies themselves.

This is a unique and remarkable book – perhaps the most extraordinary volume that it has been my privilege to supervise for publication. I hope it will bring lasting pleasure and happy memories to those who are already familiar with the fairy world, and, for those who have not as yet been granted that privilege, I hope this book will bring some illumination.

TERRY JONES
London, February 1994

July 6th 1895. Nanna wuldnt bleive me. Effie wuldnt bleivg me. Auntie Mercy wuldnt bli bleive me. But i got one. Now they.ve goX to bleive me.

July 7th 1895. I showd my ffaifaerey to Effie but she sed Nanna wuld Be cross bekaws my book is for pressing flowers in not faereys so i wont show it to anybody I am going to fill my Book up with faereys so ther ..

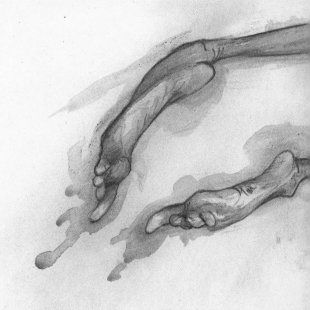

July 8th 1895 · I cort another faerey. It was flying passed my window but i was too quick for it it didnt see me cuming up behind it But i only cort a bit of it.

Aug 10th 1896. I new ther was faereys behind
the pottingshed. So i went and sat very still with
my book open in my lap and the faereys was
curius and ~~tingr~~ inkwizitf and they all came round
to look at me and one landed on my book and i
went SNAP! I banged the book shut and i
cort the faerey it is a reelly Bewtiful one.
I like it best.

Aug 12th 1896. I cort another faerey todday. But it luks very angry. I wonder if it was looking for the other faerey i cort? Perhaps is the King of the Faereys luking for his dorter or the Queen of the Faereys. But i don't care. I like collecting faereys. I am going to collect all the faereys in my Book.

Aug 8th 1899. It has been three years since I last saw a ~~funny~~ fairy. I was beginning to think I would ~~never~~ never see one agane. But I was down by the potting shed and suddenly I saw one. I crept up behind it and opened my book and SMACK! I caught it! It's a funny looking one. I think it must be a goblin or a elf.

Aug 11th 1899. A great many faeries came buzzing round me todday. They seemed quite ~~extre~~ excited and kept glaring at me and flying right up my nose. But I still caught one. I am going to call her Florizal. She is an young fairy who was a little bit more daring than the rest. I wonder what she did in Fairy Land, and how old she was? Perhaps she was ten years old - perhaps thirty - perhaps thirty thousand. It's hard to know what is old with fairies.

Here is the Story of Florizal The Nosey Fairy..

There is nothing she would not stick her nose into. If you left the milk out at night - as like as not, you'd find Florizal floating in it in the morning.

"Help me out," she would say, "for the sides of this jug are too steep and slippery and my wings are all soggy with milk."

"Will you grant me three wishes if I do?" said the little girl.

"I can't do three wishes," replied Florizal, "because I left my wand behind, but I can grant one."

"That will do," said the ~~little~~ little girl, and she put a straw into the milk and the fairy climbed up it. Then the little girl gave Florizal a wash in her own wash basin. She made a shower with a tea strainer and Florizal washed all the milk out of her wings and rule-book. (Fairies always carry a rule book with them - especially if they are only apprentice fairies like Florizal.) Then the little girl sat the fairy in front of the fire and dried her off. And all the time Florizal kept asking: "What's that burning in the grate? Where do you keep your magic powder? How do you fly anywhere? What's the name of your king? Who do you look like? Why do you go to bed at night?" and so on and so forth. And the little girl tried to answer her as best she could.

Then when she had quite dried the fairy and her wings were ~~at~~ all shimmering a ready to fly, the little girl said to Florizal:

"Now can I have my wish?"

"Oh!" said Florizal, "I said I could grant one wish, but never said it was _your_ wish! It's _my_ wish! And I wish I was out of here!" And she disappeared - like a bubble bursts - ~~and~~ and all that was left of Florizal The Nosey Fairy was a little wet patch on the rug.

For I forgot to tell you - Florizal was not only a nosey fairy she was also a very tricksy one as well.

The End.

July 15th 1902. I have been thinking that perhaps the fairies have been avoiding me, for I certainly have seen neither wing nor wand of them for some years. Sometimes I open my book of pressed fairies and I can hardly believe what I am looking at. Did I really see these creatures flying around my head? Did I really catch them in my book? Where have they gone? Have I lost the ability to see them forever?

Many times I have gone down to the potting-shed and sat there still as still and yet I have seen nothing.

Sometimes I have <u>felt</u> fairies around me – but nothing more.

But today something amazing happened.

I was down behind the potting-shed, when I spotted a little window I had never noticed before. I looked through it and could hardly believe my eyes! The inside of the potting-shed looked quite different through that window. It was all neat and tidy, and there was a little scrap of rug, and two chairs and a strange black stove – in fact just like I'd always longed to have it.

I squeezed through the little window and into the potting-shed. A fire was burning in the stove. How strange! The potting-shed was usually full of broken pots and dead tomatoes, and a few old wooden boxes full of soil. But now there was a kitchen dresser against the wall, and a book on the shelf.

I was just going to look at the book, when the kettle on the stove started to whistle. So instead I took it off the stove and filled the teapot that suddenly appeared on the table. Then a cup appeared and a jug of milk. "I suppose I might as well have a cup of tea," I said to myself. But it was the strangest tasting tea I ever did drink, and afterwards I felt quite drowsy... In fact I think I must have sat in that cosy chair and fallen asleep, for the next minute it was dark.

There was a candle burning on the dresser. When I went across to it I saw that the book was now open. So I picked it up and read what was written on the page. It said:

"The Fairy Call
A spell for summoning the fairies.

Sit where the cat sits. Cross your toes.
Close your eyes. And smell a rose.
"Then say under your breath:
I believe in fairies, sure as death."

Gladflykins! Gladtrypins!
Gutterpuss and Cass!
Come to me fairily
Each lad and lass!"

Just at that moment, I heard my Governess calling from the house, and I knew I was in trouble. I rushed to the door of the potting-shed and tried to open it. But it seemed to be locked, which is odd, because the potting-shed door is never locked. And when I peered through the keyhole I saw... Dear Diary, I cannot even tell you what I saw! It was... perhaps one day I will write it down, but just now I can't...

I climbed out of the window, but unluckily I dropped the book back inside as I was jumping out. "I'll get it tomorrow," I thought, and ran up to the house. She really was very angry with me. She thought I had run away, because it was so late and I had been gone so long. I didn't get any supper.

July 16th 1902. This morning, as soon as ever I had finished my lessons, I ran down to the potting-shed, but there was a mystery. I could not find the little window through which I'd climbed only yesterday. It was quite quite vanished - as if it had never been. I almost cried. But I said to myself: "Come come! This will never do! Sir Walter would never have sat down and cried!" Then it suddenly occurred to me that I could remember the spell - clear as daylight!

So I fetched my Pressed Fairy Book and my chair and sat behind the shed and said the spell. I sat and waited and waited, but nothing happened. Then I realised I was doing it all wrong. I had to do what the spell said. I had to sit where the cat sits and smell a rose and all that.

The cat sits in the aubrietia. So I got a rose, sat amongst the aubrietia and shut my eyes. Before you could say Simpkin-Spilikins, I heard tiny sounds like sugar cubes falling in a well, and tiny laughter and music no louder than a mouse's breath. I opened my eyes and there all around me on the grass and in the air were the fairies. They had returned to me after all these years.

This is the one I got this time. She is a funny little thing. I think her name must be Mothcatcher. She is a little lop-sided creature. No doubt she casts spells on chickens and on the legs of dogs. It is she who turns biscuits soggy when you dip them in your cocoa for only a second, and it is she who makes those mysterious holes that appear in your pinafore, when your Governess had it darned only the other day. I think she looks rather nervous.

July 18th 1902. The fairies didn't come yesterday. But they came today, and I caught two! One of them is called Mogcracker and the other Skamperdans. They are both mischief-makers and like getting girls into trouble. Mogcracker will take the lessons that you finished last night and got all the sums right, and make them all wrong by the morning. She gets your essays and puts all the spelling out, when you'd spelt it perfectly correctly. Skamperdans never wears her drawers. And that's why she's always stealing yours. And stockings too. She creeps around your room just out of sight, and snatches them the moment you have put them down and turned your back.

Aug 22nd 1902. A terrible shock today! I found Auntie Mercy rummaging around behind the big steamer trunk in the attic. That's where I hide this book. It's the only safe place in the house because generally no one goes up there except Ettie and me and sometimes Cousin Nicholas, but he doesn't count because he's a boy and doesn't believe in anything.

My heart jumped into my mouth and felt so frightened I almost couldn't speak, but suddenly I heard myself saying:

"Oh Auntie Mercy, is there anything I can get for you? It is terribley dirty and dusty up here you know, and you are dressed in your Sunday petticoats and Father's old silk hat, you surely don't want to get them dirty do you?"

Aunty Mercy stopped and looked round at me. She had big black smudges over her nose and cheeks, and I almost laughed out loud in her face which is a terribly rude thing to do and you must never do it to Auntie Mercy.

Well Auntie Mercy turned and frowned and said: "Don't believe in fairies."

I thought it was all up. Not that Auntie Mercy would stop me, of course, but she would be bound to tell my Governess and then goodness knows what evils would befall.

"Oh, Auntie Mercy," I said. "You must never say that. Don't you know that every time you say that a fairy dies?"

"Don't believe in fairies," she repeated.

It was only then that I noticed she had a book in her hand. Oh my goodness! ... My Pressed Fairy Book!

"Would you like me to read to you?" I asked, holding out my hand for the book. But Auntie Mercy had run to the little window in the attic and she suddenly opened it and before I could stop her she had thrown my book out so that it fell down right into the drive where the servants were preparing the carriage for my parents.

Now all was indeed lost! I ran down the stairs, hoping against hope that I would reach my precious book before any of the servants had a chance to notice it.

But when I arrived at the front door, Barker already had the book in his hands and was looking through its pages. As soon as he saw me, he hid it behind his back.

"What is that you have there, Barker?" I said, trying not to sound too anxious.

"It's nothing, Miss," he replied, looking rather ruffled.

"Oh but I think it is, Barker," I said. "And I think it belongs to me."

"Indeed I'm sure it doesn't, Miss," he said. But I was firm with him.

Barker gave me a strange look. I thought: he knows my secret! He hates me! And I quite thought he was going to take my book then and there and show my Governess. But he didn't, in fact the strangest thing happened.

I stamped my foot and said: "Barker! I really do insist that you give me that book at once or I shall be forced to complain about your behaviour to Fielding!"

At this point Barker turned bright red. "Indeed, Miss, I am sure this book is… "

"Give it to me Barker!" ∴

Then very reluctantly he handed me the book… But what were my feelings when I realised that indeed it was not my book. It was a book I had never seen before! However I pretended that it was the book I thought it was, and I took it and thanked Barker and told him that it was a very special book to me. Then I fled indoors back to my own room.

Dear Diary, imagine my horror when I sat on my bed and opened the book and discovered… Well I can hardly write down what it was… It was called A Thousand And One Arabian Nights. It apparently consisted of many stories but they were illustrated with a series of pictures which I cannot describe to you. Suffice it to say that they showed ladies and gentlemen doing well… I have no words for it… things! I blushed as I turned the pages and felt quite sick. This was the book I had claimed to Barker was mine! How would I ever be able to look that man in the eye again! I burst into tears on my bed, and cried with shame and vexation.

I ran back to the attic and searched for my book of pressed fairies but then came the worst thing of all — it had vanished!

Aug 23rd 1902. I have disposed of that dreadful book. I have still not found my Pressed Fairy Book. And I wonder how did that other book come to be there, I wonder? It certainly hadn't been there before, and Auntie Mercy would certainly never have taken it there. It is a mystery. I got my ordinary flower pressing book and caught another fairy today. Probably just a goblin.

13th Jan 1903. Today is my fifteenth birthday. I am grown-up at last. Mamma and Pappa invited me to have supper with them. It felt very strange. Mamma gave me a toasting fork and a pair of white gloves. Governess gave me a copy of The Household Compendium – an invaluable guide to all householders – and so of little interest to me. Cousin Nicholas gave me a photographic camera.

As I was getting into bed, I noticed a small fairy sitting under the wardrobe. It was crying. I bent down and picked it up! It was so upset it hardly seemed to notice, or care. I set it down on the washstand and examined it. One wing appeared to be broken. It had little marks on its dress and its wand was bent.

"What's the matter?" I asked. But it just went on sobbing its heart out. This was the first time I had ever spoken to a fairy, so I said: "What is your name?"

It looked up at me for a moment and then mumbled something like: "Pipskintinkle." But I couldn't get another word out of it. So I got out my flower pressing book and SNAP! I got it ∴

1st Feb 1903. A big argument with Cousin Nicholas about fairies. He said I was stupid to believe in such rubbish. I said that he would change his tune if I could prove to him that they exist. He said I couldn't. So I went up to the attic to find my flower pressing book. But now I couldn't find that either. It had disappeared – just like my Pressed Fairy Book! I searched the attic through and through but it had just vanished!

Cousin Nicholas kept laughing at me. He really is an opinionated young man. I said I could prove it to him and that I would take a photograph of some fairies and then that would prove it. So he said he would help me. But I told him it would be no use; that the fairies wouldn't come while he was there. But he insisted.

So we sat behind the potting-shed. I got another book and sat very very still. Presently I heard the little voices and giggling and laughing, but I could not see anything. Cousin Nicholas sat very still. He could not hear anything, he said later. Then, suddenly I saw one hovering just in front of my nose. "There!" I shouted and Cousin Nicholas took a photograph as I clapped the book shut. SNAP! ∴ Unfortunately the fairy got away. "But there was nothing there" he said. "Yes there was," I replied. "It was just you couldn't see it." I wonder if the camera saw it..

23rd Feb 1903. I have finally got the photograph developed. And I can hardly contain my excitement! There on the photograph is the fairy! Now I have proof. Nobody can call me stupid or foolish again – or accuse me of making up stories like my Governess used to do! I can show the world that there really are fairies. Even Cousin Nicholas. But, unfortunately he is away at school again.

1st March 1903. The first person I showed the photograph to was Barker. This was a mistake. He just grinned and said I was a clever little pixie. The stupid dolt of a man. Why did I show it to him?

Finally I worked up my courage and showed it to my Governess. She is a new one. She seemed very interested and wanted to know how I had done it. I said: "It is a photograph." "Yes," she replied, "But how did you make it look as if there is a fairy leaping out of your book?" I told her it was a real fairy and she went very quiet and I was later summoned to appear before my father.

I was so nervous. It is a month or more since I last spoke to Him. He had the photograph already when I approached him. He seemed quite calm, but when I repeated to him what it was he grew very angry and told me I was a wicked girl for persisting in such untruths. Finally he sent me to my room and I was to stay there until I could distinguish fact from fiction. Oh! The injustice of it all!

If only I could find my Pressed Fairy Book, I could prove it to them. But it is still lost ⁘

2nd March 1903. The most unfair fate! My father has taken the photograph of the fairy and locked it in his desk. He says I am not to have it back as long as I persist in my stories. He has also taken away my camera. What am I to do?

I ~~was~~ wrote to Cousin Nicholas.

8th March 1903. This morning I received a letter from Cousin Nicholas. He said I should steal the photograph from my father's study and send it to a newspaper. I wrote back that I should not do anything so vulgar.

I fear Cousin Nicholas betrays a coarseness of mind. Perhaps it would be better to have less to do with him in future ...

{These last entries were written on separate sheets of paper and inserted in the main volume – Ed.}

Nov 23rd 1903. Today Auntie Mercy died. We were all upstairs crying and she died in her room about 3 o'clock. The Doctor said it was very peaceful.

It is a curious thing but today I also found - at long long last - my Pressed Fairy Book. It was perfectly safe and not damaged in any way. But the most curious thing was where I found it. It was behind the steamer trunk in the attic where I had always kept it. And yet I had looked there time and time again and it had not been there.

But the strangest thing was that there were several new fairies pressed in the book! Who had done it? Certainly not Auntie Mercy. I had told no one about it. I cannot understand it. Perhaps the fairies themselves did it? But why would they press their own kind?

I opened these pages with trembling hands. And now I have a terrible confession to make. As I looked at the familiar faces of my fairies I was suddenly overwhelmed with remorse. As I thought of these dear little creatures and I imagined the end to which I had brought them, I suddenly felt a strong sensation of guilt sweep over me, and I went red as the hearth rug. How could I have done this? Surely I was the cause of much pain and anguish to these dear little things that I loved so much! Why had it never occurred to me before? Was I just a heartless little girl with no feelings?

My mind was thus in a state of such perturbation, that I know not how long I had been sitting there, when suddenly - to my astonishment - I saw a little figure hovering in the air but a few inches from the book which lay upon my lap.

And then my astonishment was complete, when the fairy spoke to me.

"Top of the dew!" it said. "My name is Tuppence. And I have come to test you on your Latin irregular verbs!"

At this, it landed on the open pages of my book, and... I don't know why, nor can I now offer any defence for what I did... but it was as if the old habit were too strong. I simply could not help myself. The moment its little feet alighted on the page I banged the book shut on it and I heard the familiar little shriek and the slight squashing sound as I pressed the book shut harder and harder.

Then it all went quiet. I looked around the room. Everything was perfectly normal. The clock was ticking on the shelf above the ottoman. My old nightgown was thrown across the back of the chair just where I had been told not to leave it. The fire in the grate crackled and fizzed with new wood. And yet I felt like a murderess. I thought my hands were stained with blood. They looked red - and yet I knew that it was my fancy, for fairy blood is never red. For a moment I thought I could hear other fairies around me. Perhaps they will seek retribution! Perhaps they will try to get their own back on me?

'For the
first time I felt
afraid. I felt uncertain
of this whole mysterious
world into which I have
had such glimpses. And
yet... if I could hear
anything... it was tiny cheers!
Impossible!
    I put the book down and
backed away to the other side
of the room. Suddenly cold
all over. I vowed I would
never ever look in my
Pressed Fairy Book
again!

{There follows a gap of three years before the next entry - Ed.}

Dec 3rd 1906 It is three years since I caught my last fairy. I have finally worked up the courage to open my Pressed Fairy Book. I opened it boldly at the last pressing... the fairy who said her name was Tuppence. Strangely I no longer felt guilty nor afraid. And when I looked at this last pressed fairy, it seemed to me that there was something odd, but I could not put my finger on it. Perhaps it did not look quite as afraid as the others. That familiar glint of horror and panic was missing from its eyes. But perhaps that is just my fancy again...

At this moment a truly odd thing happened – I had hardly been looking at the book for a minute when I heard a rude noise just behind my right ear. I thought perhaps it was Cousin Nicholas playing tricks on me and I turned around with a laugh to snap the book in his face. Imagine my surprise, then, when I found myself facing a nasty-looking little goblin, who was standing on the back of my chair blowing "raspberries" and sticking his tongue out at me. But all I had was a glimpse of him, for I was too late to stop the book snapping shut and he was gone! There was the usual squish and I at once reopened the book. There was the rude little beast – half-squashed on the page, but still sitting up and making nasty faces at me.

"Yoh Hoo! Fish-face!" it said, and then added an extremely impolite remark about my under garments, which it would not be seemly to repeat here. I therefore had little compunction in slamming the book shut on the beastly little creature and pressing the pages down as hard as I possibly could. And I didn't stop even though I could hear it squeaking and yelling. However, the next moment I was shrieking as well, for I could feel something grasping one of my fingers, and I realised that one of the creature's hands had not been caught in the book and was now waggling around free. It gave my finger the most dreadful tweak, but I went on pressing with all my strength, and eventually I heard the squeaks grow fainter and the hand finally stopped waving about and went limp. I confess, I felt a little weak at the knees. But my ordeal was not over yet. For when I opened up the book, to see what sort of impression I had obtained, I found the most gruesome and disgusting sight.

I resolved never to press fairies ever again.

4th Dec 1906. Today I caught two more goblins. They really are horrid little creatures, and I have absolutely no regrets about catching them. One of them made an awful mess on my dress, however, and I had to pretend to my new Governess that I had spilt some paint on myself. I am sure it did it deliberately.

Today was also remarkable in another way. Cousin Nicholas arrived by the afternoon train. He came up to my room where I was working, and gave me an envelope. In it was the photograph I had taken all those years ago.

He would not tell me how he had obtained it, but begged for permission to publish it in the monthly journal for which he is now working. No matter how I resisted the idea, he found some way of countering my doubts, and I eventually gave my reluctant permission, save that my name be in no way connected to its publication.

At this moment, Cousin Nicholas put his arm around my waist and kissed me in a way that quite astonished me! I asked him what he thought he meant by taking such liberties. Whereupon he smiled and said: "I had always been a bit of a cold fish" or some such nonsense.

I began to wonder whether I had done right by allowing him to publish the old photograph.

5th Dec 1906. Caught a beautiful specimen today. A large painted fairy that seemed to fly by so slowly it was almost asking to be pressed.

I am glad I did not show my Pressed Fairy Book to Nicholas. I do not understand him at the moment. He seems to be very moody.

Perhaps I will show it to him one day.

7th Dec 1906. Surrounded by fairies in Church today.
Some of them very insolent and provoking. I could not
help snapping my prayer book at them. Caught one,
but in future I shall bring my Pressed Fairy Book
to Church with me.

But GOD from infant tongues
On earth receiveth praise;
We then our cheerful songs
In sweet accord will raise:
Alleluia!
We too will sing
To GOD our King
Alleluia!

O Blessed LORD, Thy
To us Thy babes imp
And teach us in our
To know Thee as Th
Alleluia
Then sha
To GOD
Alle

O may Th
Spread all the
And all with
Uplift the jo
All
All then st
To GOD the
Alleluia

"Jesus . . . took a chil
337   by Him

THERE 's a Friend for little children
Above the bright blue sky,
A Friend Who never changes,
Whose love will never die;
Our earthly friends may fail us,
And change with changing years,
This Friend is always worthy
Of that dear Name He bears.

There 's a rest for little children
Above the bright blue sky,
Who love the Blessed Saviour,
And to the FATHER cry;
A rest from every turmoil
From sin and sorrow free,
Where every little pilgrim
Shall rest eternally.

There 's a home for little children
Above the bright blue sky,
Where Jesus reigns
A home of peace an
No home on earth is like
Nor can with it compare;
For every one is happy,
Nor could be happier, there.

There 's a crown for little children
Above the bright blue sky,
And all who look for JESUS
Shall wear it by and by;
A crown of brightest glory,
Which He will then bestow
On those who found His favour
And loved His Name below.

There 's a song for little children
Above the bright blue sky,
A song that will not weary,
Though sung continually:

song which even Angels
Can never, never sing;
They know not CHRIST as Saviour,
But worship Him as King.

There 's a robe for little children
Above the bright blue sky;
A harp of sweetest music,
palms of victory.
A above is treasured
And d in CHRIST alone;
rant Thy little children
Thee as their own. Amen.

(ower of God, as dear

end Thy bless-
red here, [ing
confessing,
loving,
pure;
David, proving,
death endure.

oly SA Who in meekness
Didst safe a Child to be,
Guide steps, and help their
weak
Bless and make them like to Thee:
Bear Thy lambs, when they are weary,
In Thine Arms and at Thy Breast;
Through life's desert dry and dreary,
ring them to Thy heavenly rest.

Spread Thy golden pinions o'er them,
HOLY SPIRIT, from above,
Guide them, lead them, go before
them,
Give them peace and joy and love
the temple HOLY SPIRIT,
ay they with Thy glory shine,
immortal inherit,
And for e Thine. Amen.

not lay to offer the first of
39   thy ripe fruits."

AIR waved the golden corn
In Canaan's pleasant land,
When full of joy, some shining morn,
Went forth the reaper-band.

To GOD so good and great
Their cheerful thanks they pour:
Then carry to His temple-gate
The choicest of their store.

Like Israel, LORD, we give
Our earliest fruits to Thee,
And pray that, long as we shall live
We may Thy children be.

Thine is our youthful prime,
And life and all its powers;
Be with us in our morning time,
And bless our evening hours.

5th Jan 1907. Disaster! "The Regular" came out today with my fairy photograph emblazoned on the first page, accompanied by a long article in which I am not only named as the photographer, but am hailed as an authority on Fairy Lore and cited as a believer in fairies, goblins, gnomes, elves and pixies. I shall become a laughing-stock. I shall never speak to Cousin Nicholas ever again.

Caught such a strange creature today. I do not know what kind of a fairy it could be.

7th Jan 1907. A fairy called Findlefick flew in my window and sat on the end of my bed this morning.

"Would you like to take my photograph?" It asked. So I set up my camera and prepared the plates. But the moment I took off the lens cap the beastly little thing made rude gestures at me. I told it that it must sit still — otherwise I could not photograph it. So Findlefick sat still and I got out my book and —

SNAP! The vain thing was so busy posing it did not even notice me creeping up behind it ..

12th Jan 1907. It is as I feared. "The Regular" is full of letters today making fun of my photograph and, of course, of me. It is so humiliating. There were one or two readers, however, who seemed to be impressed and wished to meet me. I shall have nothing to do with them ofcourse.

Got three fairies and two goblins this afternoon! They have never been so easy to catch!

SNAP! SNAP! SQUASH!

I went! It was very exciting!

13th Jan 1907. Cousin Nicholas came this morning and proposed marriage to me! Did you ever hear of such a thing? I told him not to be so ridiculous. He seemed quite upset. I'm sure I don't know why. He knows how I feel about him. How could I tolerate someone who laughs at me behind my back? Besides what do I want to have to do with men? They have hair in their ears!

Several newspapermen were round the house this morning pestering me. I shall have to go away. I cannot bear all this. My only consolation is my fairies. Got four today, a goblin, and what I think may be my first pixie!

1st May 1907. <u>Napoli, Italy</u>. I have escaped! It is beautiful. But even here I am surrounded by my fairy friends. This one came and hovered over my bed. I keep my book under the bedclothes and was able to surprise it.

2nd May 1907. Lord Crowley asked for my hand in marriage this morning. Such arrogance! We only met two months ago, and I scarcely think I have formed any attachment to him — nor, indeed, do I imagine that he could believe that I had! And yet there he was on his knees trying to grasp my hand in his. The most terrible shudder of revulsion ran through my veins as I remembered that book so long ago, and I imagined the depictions within it of men and women caressing in the most lewd and abandoned manner — and then I thought of myself and this gross man in similar contact ... oh my blood runs cold just to think of it! Lord Crowley has more hair in his ears than anyone I know.

My fairy collection grows every day! But I am not at all sure that these Italian fairies are quite proper. They seem to have a leering quality about them that I do not at all like.

10th May 1907. More Italian fairies. They seem to be almost showing off. I am not sure I like them.

15th May 1907. I do not know when I have been so vexed and horrified. I had been feeling rather unwell, and retired to my bed early, when I heard a knock on the door. My chambermaid opened it and announced Lord Crowley wished to speak to me. I was about to say no, when in he walked bold as brass. To my horror Mathilda withdrew at the same moment, saying she had some pressing business downstairs. "Mathilda!" I shouted. But the hussey was gone—leaving me alone in my bedroom with a man! What should I have done?

At this moment my astonishment was completed by the appearance of a couple of fairies, hovering in the air just behind Lord Crowley's shoulder. I confess, that at their appearance I must have smiled, for they certainly looked properly comic. Thus the damage was done! Lord Crowley took my smile as a hint of encouragement, and in no time, he had sprung to my bedside and seized me in his arms crying: "My darling! I knew you wanted me to come!"

Imagine my indignation and despair. As I felt his moustachios covering my mouth, I almost choked, and then as I gasped for air, I caught sight of the most ludicrous display. The two fairies were performing a rediculous pantomime of his Lordship behind his back. One of them was pretending to be me and the other Lord Crowley—complete with vast whiskers made from the cats' tail. Unawares of all this, Lord Crowley pressed me to his breast and a gasp of laughter escaped me. This the stupid man took as further encouragement! "Yes! Yes!" he cried. "Your happiness is my happiness!" Oh misery! Before I knew what was happening, he had buried his face in my nightdress and was trying to put his disgusting hands upon my body!

I will not go into further details of this most unhappy night. Suffice it to say that those wicked fairies flew around me, tickling me and touching me with their wicked little hands so that I cried out with laughter, or gasped for breath on more than one occassion thus fuelling His Lordship in his mistaken impression that I was encouraging him!

Indeed, every time I raised my hands to strike the beastly fellow or to push him away from me, one or other of those naughty fairy folk would tickle me under the arms so that I shrieked with laughter and pulled my arms back. Whereupon His Lordship kept shouting: "That's it! Give me the reins! Saddle her up! Now the water jump!" and so forth. The man was clearly quite out of his mind.

How long this ordeal continued, I am not sure. But I grew weak and trembling with my exertions and one of those impudent fairies seemed to be right inside me – tickling me from within so that I could scarce think and scarce knew what was going on.

When I came to myself, I was lying alone in my bed. To my infinite relief, His Lordship had gone, but the two fairies were sitting on the end of my bed. They were grinning, though they looked dischevelled.

"Go away!" I shouted at them. But they just turned around and bared their bottoms at me! Whereupon I seized up my book and BLATT! I got them both in one smack. Serve them right. Though it is so indecent a picture that I can now scarcely look into my own precious book, let alone invite others to gaze upon it!

16th May 1907. Stayed in my bed all day.

17th May 1907. Greatly troubled by fairies today. As I descended the main staircase of the Villa Carnale this morning, I saw what I took to be a small gremlin, sitting on the lower newel post. As I passed by it, trying to ignore it, I heard it whisper: "Hairy ears!" at me. I blushed bright red, I am sure, and I could not stop my hand going to my ears to feel if I had indeed begun to sprout such loathsome hair. But all my hand found was the little gremlin, which had somehow leapt onto my shoulder without my noticing and was now lodged in my ear. Do what I could I could not remove it. It just got deeper and deeper.

At this moment, I turned into the morning room and came face to face with the person I least wished to see in all the world – Lord Crowley. He seemed almost as taken aback as I, but then he bowed, seized my hand and kissed it several times. Then as several more house guests began to arrive, he whispered: "Tonight, my love?"

Before I could reprove him for his insolence my misery was complete. The little gremlin, seated in my ear, must have stuck its head out, and in a perfect mimic of my voice it said: "Oh yes, my dear! I cannot wait!"

Whereupon, Lord Crowley kissed my hand and was gone, and I was surrounded by Lord and Lady Kirkubright and the Sloanes, before I could even speak a word. And then there was that sly little gremlin performing a jig on Lady Sloane's cloche. I scowled at it, and – oh dear – Lady Sloane thought I was in an ill temper with her and refused to speak to me for the rest of the day. I shall, however, lock my door, and instruct Mathilda to remain with me all night.

18th May 1907. I begin to wonder whether the fairies are taking their revenge upon me. The one thing I am certain of is that last night was all their fault. After my careful instructions nothing went according to plan. Mathilda apparently took some sleeping drug and remained in her own room fast asleep, where I was unable to rouse her. I did indeed think of sleeping the night in her bed, but the thought that I could at least lock the door encouraged me to return to my own bedroom. There I carefully turned the key in the lock and placed the key upon the mantlepiece.

About half an hour later, I heard a little scrabbling noise, and tip-toeing over to the door, I saw a little gremlin creature wriggling out of the keyhole. It jumped down onto the carpet and performed a rude little dance in front of me. "Go away!" I cried more than once. But the little thing suddenly shrank itself down so I could hardly see it and then leapt towards my face!

At the same time, I heard a tap on the door. "Mathilda?" I whispered. But the door opened and in slipped none other than... Lord Crowley!

I tried to exclaim: "Lord Crowley! There has been a dreadful mistake!" But to my dismay I found that the little gremlin had jumped into my mouth and was now holding my tongue and twisting it this way and that against my will, so that what I said sounded more like: "Lord Crowley! I could hardly wait!"

I will draw a veil over what happened, but as soon as Lord Crowley was gone I made sure that I got that beastly little gremlin. Here he is.

I also decided that I must leave Italy on the first available boat.

3rd Sept 1907. Framlingham. I am so relieved to be free of those wretched Italian fairies. I can still scarcely credit the trouble and wickedness into which they led me. Now I am back and will be surrounded only by good English fairies: woodland nymphs and sprites and dryads. I feel the air is cleaner and sweeter already. Ah! The peaceful lanes, the green hills and the still woods! I will dedicate myself to my collection of Pressed Fairies, and forget about the horrors of my continental soujourn.

Or so I thought this morning as I stepped into the garden of the old house for the first time since my return. But I was to discover that "Italian ways" seem to have affected the fairies even in England. Oh! How can I go on collecting them? And yet how can I stop? Pressing my fairies has become such a part of my life, that I fear, were I to stop, my existence would have no more meaning. What am I saying. Perhaps I am going mad?

I was sitting in the arbour, upon the stone bench, when I heard a rustle behind me. I turned to find several fairies all dressed-up as if for a ball.

"Where are you lot going?" I asked them bold as brass.

"Wouldn't you like to know," said the first — a shameless little creature in a high laced-up bodice.

"We're dancing a Dainty-Four," said another. "Do you want to join us?"

Dear Diary, I should have known it was wrong, but what could I do? The fairies had never before invited me to be one of their number. I could hardly believe my good fortune — or what I thought was my good fortune. Of course, I was soon to realise my mistake, but it is all very well to be wise after the event.

"Yes," I replied, "I should like to very much."

"Then take this," said the fairy who wore a ring in her nose. She handed me a buttercup that was full to the brim of some potion.

"What is it?" I asked warily.

"Try it," said the fairy.

It was almost as if I were already under their spell. Even as I told myself I would regret it, I took a sip from the buttercup, and the sweetest nectar slipped around and over my tongue like a liquid glove of exquisite pleasure or pain — I could not be sure which.

"Now you are the right size," said the fairy in the hat, and sure enough, I found I was no bigger than any of them.

"So you can dance the Dainty-Four with us," said Rumbleskamps — the fairy with the ring in her nose.

They took my hand and we ran through the foxgloves and we ran through the fleur-de-lis, we ran through the horehound, the cockscomb and the dandelion. We ran out into the wide, wide wood. And there in a fairy-ring, overhung with daisies we shook off our bonnets and we shook off our pinafores, we loosened our stays and the ribbons on our camisoles, we stepped right out of our skirts and our petticoats, and we danced all as naked as the love-lies-bleeding, as bare as the baby's breath that blooms by the boulders, and we shook our shoulders at the aster and the hyacinth. We danced till we fell down — laughing to the asphodel and the jack-by-the-hedge covered us over.

I cannot account for what happened next, but I suddenly looked up and saw the Rev. Cowdrey, standing above me.

"Angelica! Angelica!" he exclaimed. "What has become of you? I had hopes to ask you to be my wife, but... oh! Angelica!"

It was at this point I realised I was stark naked, rolling on my back in the garlic mustard that grows in the wood. I had no clue where my clothes were, and as the vicar threw his cloak over me, and escorted me back to the house, I pretended to be delirious. I spent the next three days in bed.

Oh! Those wicked, wicked fairies. I am sure they did it on purpose!

But the worst of it all — Oh! The worst shame of it all was to learn of the vicar's intentions towards me! I can still hardly contain my anger and humiliation. To think that a five-guinea-a-week clergyman could think himself worthy of the daughter of the fourteenth Earl of Cottington ... even now the impertinence makes me tremble with anger.

12th Sept 1907. What am I to do? My fairy tormentors will not let me be. For I realise now, that they are tormenting me. It is deliberate. I am sure of that.

Even lying in my bed they sometimes tip-toe around me. They think I cannot see them. But I do. I open one eye just a crack and I see Dewletter or GrimThumb or CymbalTurnip ... (For I am grown so familiar with them nowadays, I even know their names) ... as they creep across my covers, giggling and nudging each other. The odious little pests. Why won't they leave me alone?

It's not as if I don't catch them! This is GrimThumb.

I sometimes pray that an Angel will come and chase them all away. But God does not seem to hear me. Perhaps there are no Angels. Only Fairies. Oh what a wicked world .... I cannot bear to think of it ...

13th Oct. 1909 Today I spoke with the Bishop. I had decided to do this a month ago, and this morning when he called, I resolved to take the plunge. I cannot tell you how fearful I was, and yet I felt there was no other help for me against the Fairies.

The Bishop was, of course, familiar with the photograph that had appeared in "The Regular" two years ago, but how was I to tell him of the things that had happened since? Or of the doubts that had assailed me in recent years? Still, since the mysterious death of my parents two years ago, he has been my spiritual adviser, and I took courage from the fact that he was a learned man and a sympathetic friend. Or so I thought.

We were seated in the morning room beside a small fire. The sunlight swept in through the window and dazzled me somewhat, so that I could not clearly see the Bishop's face. However, I had resolved to tell my story and I am not the sort of person to be put off once I have come to a decision.

"Your Grace," I began. "I feel I can confide in you as my oldest and most trusted friend."

"My dear Lady Angelica," he replied. "No-one could have your best interests more closely bound to their heart."

I shut my eyes and took a deep breath. This was the moment. I had this book – my book of Pressed Fairies – upon my lap and it gave me confidence to feel its familiar edges and smell the slight perfumed fragrance that exuded from its pages and that seemed to strengthen as my collection grew. It was time I spoke out, and for the first time since I had spoken to that wretched Cousin Nicholas, I would reveal to someone my long-held secret.

In the sun-beams I thought, for a fleeting instant, that I saw Moon Hopper fondling her breasts close to his Grace's ear, but as I looked again all I could see was dust in the air.

"Your Grace," I began again, "since I was a small child..."

And so I told him of my first experiences with the Fairies, I told him of Florizal, the Nosey Fairy, of the Fairy Call, of the Mischief-makers. I told him about Auntie Mercy and the disappearance of my precious book, of Pipskintinkle and Tuppence, of the way the Fairies seemed to grow bolder and seemed to provoke me in to pressing them. I then carefully broached the subject of the Italian fairies, and the shameful way in which they behaved towards me at the Villa Carnale, and I was just leading on to the distressing way in which they have tormented me ever since my return to England, when to my utter surprise I found his Grace seizing my hand in his and whispering to me in an urgent voice:

"Oh! Lady Angelica! Yes! They torment me too! Those little fairies!"

Upon my faith, I do believe the man had taken leave of his senses! I moved out of the sunlight in order to be able to see him properly. His eyes had an unnerving intensity about them and he seemed to have dribbled on his purple front! At the same time he slipped his arms around my waist.

"Oh Lady Angelica!" he was mumbling. "It's only natural! Let yourself go! Follow the fairies! You are so beautiful! So damned beautiful! Yes! They torment me too!"

My book of Pressed Fairies fell to the floor. I tried to beat him off, but it is difficult to strike one's spiritual adviser—particularly when he is the Bishop of Stoke and Cherwell.

"There is only one way to defeat the fairies!" he sounded more as if he were moaning than talking. "Give in! Do what they urge you to!" And His Grace suddenly put his tongue into my mouth!

I do not know which surprised me the most — the fact of suddenly having someone else's tongue in my mouth or the fact that it was a tongue that hitherto I had only glimpsed in the course of delivering sermons on the denial of the flesh and the pleasures of abstinence.

"Your Grace!" I managed to say, but he was already fumbling with my corsage. "Those fairies! They lead me a merry dance I can tell you! Ah! Your breasts are whiter than a five-pound note!"

"Let me show them to you!" I cried.

"I can see them! I can see them!" He seemed to be almost hysterical.

"I mean the fairies," I said and I groped for my book on the floor beside the chair. I had just got my fingers around it, when there was a knock at the door. The Bishop leapt to his feet as if he had been electrocuted. I struggled to adjust my dress, but the bodice was torn and several buttons were missing.

However, I managed to say: "Enter" and Fielding came in to inform His Grace that his carriage was now ready.

The Bishop's face was as purple as his stock, but he managed to pull himself together and make his reply in a reasonably calm voice. As he reached the door, he turned and gave me a final bow, and then ... in the flash of sunlight as he stood erect once more, I saw Moon Hopper skip from his dog collar and slide down his cassock into an aspidistra pot. There was something so comical about the Bishop that I almost felt sorry for him.

That night two fairies whom I had never seen before came and sat at the end of my bed. They just sat there looking at me without saying anything. At length I said:

"Why don't you all leave me alone? What do you all want?"

"We thought you'd never ask," they said.

"Well? What is it?" I asked.

"You've got to guess," they said.

I hesitated. When I tried to speak, it only came out as a whisper: "Revenge. That's what you want isn't it?"

The two creatures burst into peals of laughter and jumped into the air around my head.

"Angelica! Angelica!" they cried, "You never understood!" And then they were gone before I could ask them anything more.

5th Dec 1909. Fairies thick and fast around my bed, in my wardrobe, under my washstand. What has got into them? They are like dust in the air.

"Go away! Shoo!"

I ran around my bedroom, snapping my book at them and catching them by the armful. Dingle Fritter, Gooseberry Humple, Tiger Get-By, Lone Folding, Zimber Quattor ... I recognise so many of them now and yet ... SNAP! I catch them between my pages by the dozen! By the end of it I can hardly shut the book!

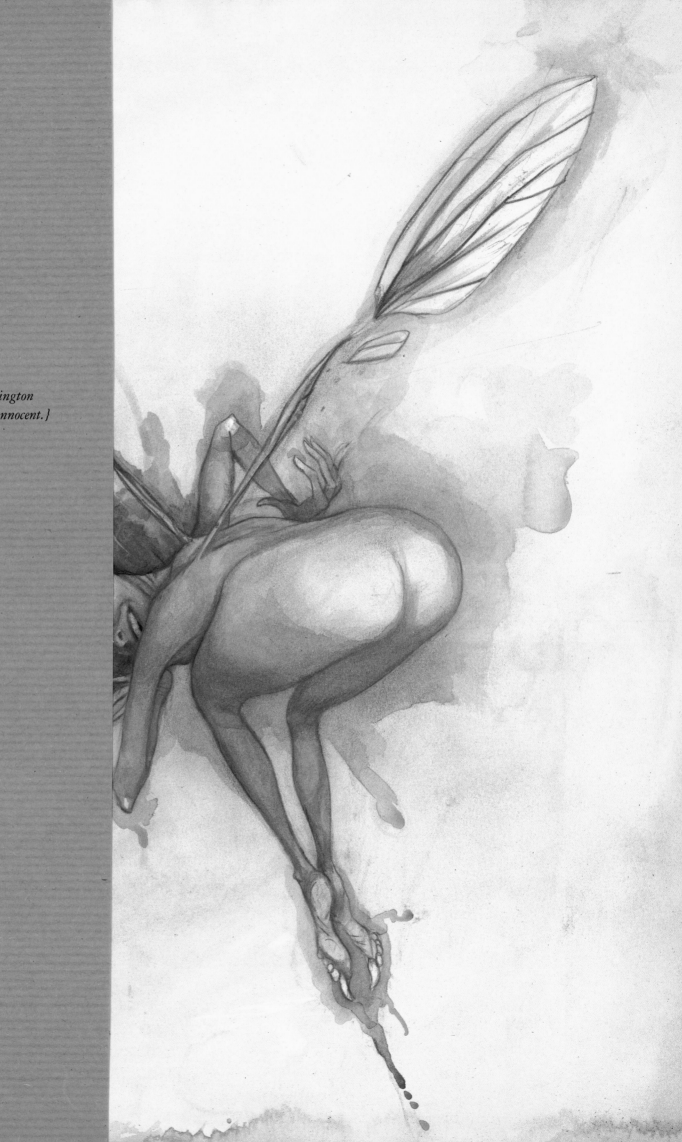

6th Dec 1909 · No fairies today ·

7th Dec 1910 · Not a single fairy all [...]
has happened? I miss them.

Dec · 1912 · I fear the fairies have g[...]
good · All I can do is turn the pages of [...]
remember them all ···

Angelica Cottington

{The fairies never seem to have visited Lady Cottington again. She never married although s[...]
from no fewer than fourteen suitors - all of them hereditary peers or men of the cloth. She turn[...]
and more retiring, choosing to live alone with her housekeeper. She died aged 103, and her P[...]
in the attic, until the house was sold to make way for a Prestige Office Block in an unspoilt [...]